Thomas Tomlinson

The Congo Treaty

Thomas Tomlinson

The Congo Treaty

ISBN/EAN: 9783337244286

Printed in Europe, USA, Canada, Australia, Japan

Cover: Foto ©Andreas Hilbeck / pixelio.de

More available books at **www.hansebooks.com**

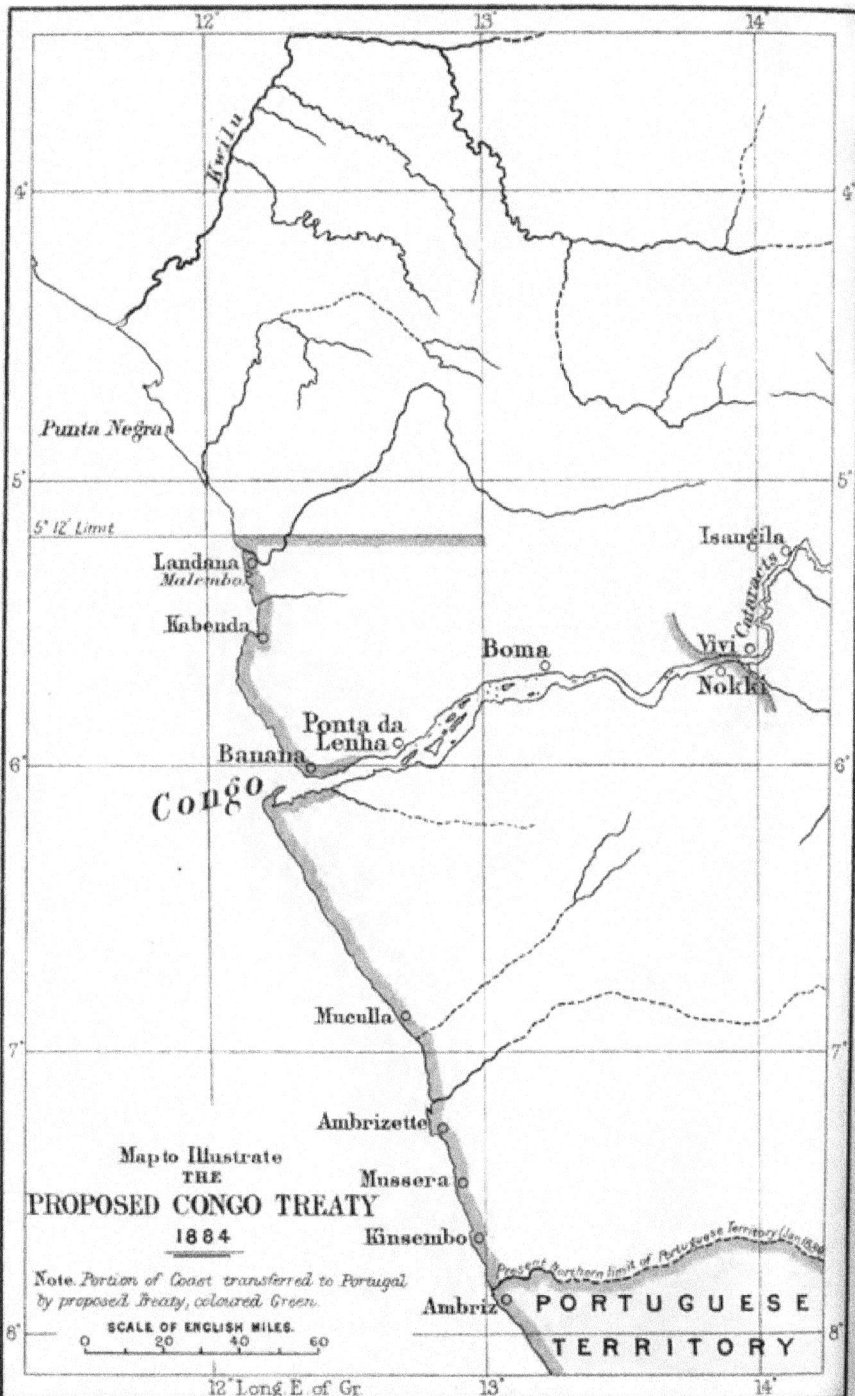

Punta Negras

5° 12' Limit

Landana
Malembo
Kabenda
Boma
Isangila
Vivi
Nokki

Ponta da
Lenha
Banana

Congo

Muculla

Ambrizette

Map to Illustrate
THE
PROPOSED CONGO TREATY
1884

Mussera

Kinsembo

Note. Portion of Coast transferred to Portugal
by proposed Treaty, coloured Green.

Present Northern limit of Portuguese Territory (Jan 1884)

SCALE OF ENGLISH MILES.

0   20   40   60

Ambriz

PORTUGUESE

TERRITORY

12° Long. E. of Gr.

THE

CONGO TREATY.

BY

THOMAS TOMLINSON, M.A.,

CHRIST CHURCH, OXFORD ;

OF THE INNER TEMPLE, BARRISTER-AT-LAW.

LONDON:

EDWARD STANFORD 55, CHARING CROSS.

1884.

THE CONGO TREATY.

At the opening of the present Session, the attention of Parliament was called to the Congo Treaty, allusion being made to the subject, in the following terms, in the Speech from the Throne:—

"An agreement has been arrived at with Portugal respecting the River Congo, and the adjacent territories. This agreement will be presented to you forthwith."

This announcement caused great interest in commercial circles, especially in the centres of the manufacturing industry of Lancashire; and much dissatisfaction and uneasiness is felt among residents and traders in the Congo district.

The negotiations which were commenced between Her Majesty's Government and the Government of Portugal in November, 1882, have resulted in the conclusion of a treaty. We now know the meaning and nature of the "agreement;" the treaty between Her Majesty and the King of Portugal, signed on the 26th of February, 1884, having been presented to Parliament, and published.*

Earnest consideration has been given to the treaty by the principal Chambers of Commerce in the country; and the effect the treaty may have on the existing trade of the Lower Congo district, and (from a wider point of view) on the commercial interests of this country, as well as on the future development of West Africa, is receiving the attention of the public. Mr. Jacob Bright shows in *The Times* of May 19th the harassing effect of the treaty on the shipping trade. He refers to the regulations affecting shipowners, and says "on reading them, one is dis-

---

* See page 46.

posed to ask, whether trade and intercourse between distant peoples are crimes, which ought to be discouraged by any means which human ingenuity can invent? The statement of Lord Granville in his letter to M. d'Antas, March 15th, 1883, 'that it would be impossible to agree to the imposition of burdens, which do not now exist,' was soon forgotten by the framers of the treaty."

Efforts were made last session, in Parliament, during the debate on a resolution moved by Mr. Jacob Bright, to place in a clear light the real facts of the Congo question. The motion was withdrawn on Mr. Gladstone promising "that the treaty should be made known to Parliament before ratification in such a way, and with the intervention of such an interval, that Parliament shall be enabled to exercise an independent judgment upon it." "I do not believe," Mr. Gladstone said, "that my honourable friend the mover of the motion has any other object or purpose in view whatever, except that which we also have. We may err in the mode of giving effect to our common wishes. Therefore, I say, he shall have an opportunity of judging of the way we propose to give effect to them before the country is finally bound by them."

Clearer language could not have been used, and we can understand that through the usual channels of information, if by no other means, Mr. Gladstone's statement must have come to the knowledge of the Portuguese Minister.

The debate in Parliament has been postponed, communications on the subject of the treaty having been re-opened with the Government of Portugal. On the 8th of May, it was stated by Mr. Gladstone in Parliament that the Government would inform the House, when these communications were brought to a conclusion.

The public interest in this subject is increasing, and we propose in this paper, briefly, to consider the Congo Treaty question. It may be useful to bring together some information relating to West Africa, and the Congo district, and opinions expressed by such authorities as Dr. Livingstone, Mr. Monteiro, and Commander Cameron are referred to.

The commercial and political aspect of the question is principally kept in view; the intention being to discuss the general purport of the treaty as it has been explained and defended by the Government.

PART I.

Livingstone, in his 'Researches in South Africa,' thus speaks of the natural richness and productions of Angola. "The fertility of the district"—he is describing the valley of the Quanza—"is marvellous to behold. All sorts of fruit trees and grapes yield their fruit twice a year, without labour or irrigation being bestowed." Of the extensive coffee plantations, found on the mountain sides in the district of Cajengo, he says, "They were not planted by the Portuguese; the Jesuit and other missionaries are known to have brought Mocha seed, and these have propagated themselves far and wide; hence the excellence of Angola coffee." We are told how pine-apples, bananas, yams, and orange-trees were, in the same way, introduced.

But he adds, "Viewing the valley as a whole, it may be said that its agricultural and pastoral riches are lying waste. Both the Portuguese and their descendants turn their attention, almost exclusively, to trade in wax and ivory, and though the country would yield any amount of corn and dairy produce, the natives live chiefly on manioc, and the Europeans purchase their flour, bread, butter, and cheese, from the Americans."

As regards means of transport, he writes: "There being no roads for wheeled conveyances, a system of compulsory carriage by porters is resorted to by the Government of Loanda."

We learn that on this line of road to the coast, as we know
is the case in very many, if not in most, parts of Africa, "calico
is the chief medium of exchange."

Livingstone says: "The Portuguese law preventing the subjects of any other nation from holding landed property, unless
they become naturalised, the country has neither the advantage
of native nor foreign enterprise, and remains very much in the
same state as in 1575. There is not a single English merchant
at Loanda, and only two American. This is the more remark-
able, as nearly all the commerce is carried on by means of
English calico brought viâ Lisbon." A more enterprising spirit
may, perhaps, some day prevail.

Some of the best informed Portuguese expressed to Livingstone their great dissatisfaction at the state of things. He tells
us " We were most kindly received by the commandant. Like
every other person of intelligence I had met, he lamented deeply
the neglect with which this fine country has been treated."

Livingstone says: "I have no hesitation in asserting that
had Angola been in the possession of England, it would now
have been yielding as much or more of the raw material for
her manufactures, as an equal extent of territory in the cotton
growing states of America. A railway from Loanda to the
valley of the Quango would secure the trade of most of the
interior of South Central Africa." It has, however, recently
been stated, we are glad to see, that the Portuguese Minister
of Marine has presented a bill to the Cortes, authorising
the Government to adjudicate upon the question of the con-
struction of a line of railway from Loanda to Ambaca in the
province of Angola. This resolution of the Portuguese Government, whether prompted or not by the prominence given here
in Parliament last year to the neglected and impoverished state
of Angola, is extremely satisfactory.

We have thus, briefly, shown the opinions of Livingstone, and
we now refer to Monteiro, who spent many years as a trader in

the Congo district, and whose ' Angola and the Congo' was published in 1875. Monteiro had personal experience of the working of the Portuguese system in the territories south of Ambritz, and at Ambritz itself; but looked hopefully to the prospects of the free Congo region.

"Since the last slave was shipped in 1868,"—Monteiro is speaking of the Congo district—" the development of produce in this part of the coast, and from the interior has been very great, and promises in a few years to be still more, and very important in amount. This will be more particularly the case when the present system ceases by which natives of the coast towns act as middle men to the natives from the interior." Monteiro observes that " from the small extent of coast comprised between Ambritz and the Congo, we have a striking example of the wonderful increase of trade and industry among the natives, since the extinction of the slave trade, and we have evidence of the great fertility of a country that, with the rudest appliances, can return such quantities of valuable produce." " About twelve years ago" (he wrote in 1875) " a very few tons with the exception of ivory, ground nuts, and copal being exported. Last year" (1874) " from Ambritz to, but not including the river Congo, the exports were—

Adansonia fibre	..	1500 tons.
Ground nuts	..	7500 „
Coffee	..	1000 „
India rubber	..	400 „

"amounting altogether in value to £300,000."

He proceeds: "This is an extremely gratifying result, from which valuable lessons are to be deduced, when we compare it with what has taken place in other parts of the coast in the immediate neighbouring country to the south in the possession of the Portuguese, and is a splendid example of the true principles by which the African race, in Africa, can be successfully civilised, and the only manner in which the riches of the west coast can be developed, and made available to the wants of the rest of the world. Trade or commerce is the great civiliser of Africa."

Monteiro then invites us to look at Loanda and the interior of the Portuguese province of Angola. He says with regard to the sad state of the country : " only a total change in the system of government, can again people the vast deserted tracts with industrious inhabitants, to cultivate its rich land ; but, I am sorry to say, a termination to the long reign of corruption that has existed in Angola, is not to be expected for years to come. As might be expected, the great peninsular obstruction and impediment of high custom-house duties, so fatal to all commercial and industrial development, is in full and vexatious force in Angola." He further says : " With the great want of roads and carriers, and other means of conveyance, either for goods into or produce from the interior, transport is very expensive, and it is evident that the levying of high import duties, besides, on all goods for trade, so enhances their value, that it becomes impossible to offer an adequate return or advantage to the native for the result of his labour or industry, or to leave much margin of profit to the merchant ; consequently the development of the country becomes completely paralysed, and the revenue of the state becomes small in proportion."

"The river Quanza," we are told, " is the gem of the Portuguese possession of Angola. South of the great river Congo, it is the only river navigable for any distance, and it is the natural highway to the most fertile, and healthy countries of the interior, navigable as far as Cambanbe."

With regard to the coffee trade, considerable business might be carried on at Loanda, but to use Monteiro's words, " the trade is shut out by the stupid and short-sighted policy of high custom-house duties on goods, and other restrictions on trade of the Portuguese authorities. Very little is cultivated. It is the product of coffee-trees growing spontaneously in the virgin forests of the second elevation. The natives, of course, have no machinery to separate the berry from the pod, these being dried in the sun, and then broken in a wooden mortar, and the husks separated by winnowing in the open air."

The effect of the occupation of Ambritz by the Portuguese, is thus described: "The Portuguese following their usual blind and absurd policy on the occupation of Ambritz, established a custom-house, and levied high duties on all goods imported. The consequence was that the foreign houses, to escape their exactions, at once removed to Kinsembo on the other side of the river Loge."

Here is one of the passages from Monteiro that was referred to in Parliament last year by Mr. Jacob Bright: "It is a great pity that Portugal should neglect, so disgracefully, her colonies, so rich in themselves, and offering such wonderful advantages in every way for colonisation and development."

As to the cost of transport on the Quanza, it was observed by Mr. Jacob Bright, that for a distance on the river of from 150 to 200 miles, as much is charged as between Liverpool and the Congo.

There are difficulties in the traders' path, which make it so essential to leave trade to feel its own way, as free as possible from restrictions; and if the Portuguese could concentrate their energy in trying to develop their own rich possessions, instead of seeking to extend along the coast, they would have plenty to do. It is observed by Monteiro, "That the natives of Angola will cultivate large quantities of produce, if they get moderately well paid for their trouble, is evidenced by the considerable exports from the country from Ambritz to the Congo, where there are no custom-houses, and also on the Quanza, where steam navigation enables goods to be sent up the country cheaply, and so to bear the almost prohibitive duties levied on them at Loanda. It is not merely the high duties, but the absurd, petty, and vexatious manner in which the whole system is worked."

But, we must pass on, to hear what information Commander Cameron can give, the latter part of whose route across the great continent was through the Portuguese possessions in West Africa; his work 'Across Africa,' was published in 1877.

"The mighty Congo," using the traveller's words, "king of all African rivers, and second only to the Amazon and Yang-tse-Kiang in the volume of its waters, has many affluents, which fork into those of the Zambesi." "The Congo would seem," Cameron says, "to offer a highway to the remotest part of the Continent."

"The whole trade of tropical Africa," he says, "is at present dependent on human beings, as beasts of burden, and valuable labour which might be profitably employed in cultivating the ground or collecting products for exportation is thus lost."

Mr. Capper, whose valuable testimony we shall refer to again, relates that he has seen an ivory caravan numbering as many as 7000 bearers.

Cameron frequently bears witness to the slave trade, and he says, "On the lines occupied by the Portuguese, especially that from Bihé to Urua and Katanga, there is a vast amount of internal slave trade; but the greater part of those captured—for they are nearly all obtained by rapine and violence—are not taken to the coast, but to Kaffir countries where they are exchanged for ivory."

Then he observes, "Having the probable extinction of ivory in view, and allowing, as all sensible people must, that legitimate commerce is the proper way to open up, and civilise a country, we must see what other lucrative sources of trade may hereafter replace that in ivory. Fortunately, we have not far to go, for the vegetable and mineral products of this marvellous land are equal in variety, value and quantity to those of the most favoured portions of the globe."

With regard to supplying labour for making roads, he observes, "when the chiefs find it more profitable to employ their subjects in their own country than to sell them as slaves, they will lose the most powerful incentive towards complying with the demands of the slave trader."

He asserts that the first step necessary for the development of the country, is the establishment of proper means of communication.

Of the capabilities of the country, Cameron says he found it "far and wide favourable for the growth and production of cotton, sugar cane, oil palm, indiarubber and tobacco." To the west of Nyangwe, on the Lualaba, or Upper Congo, he observed coffee as large as the Mocha bean, and he speaks of an opening there might be for trade in hide and beeswax. The abundant resources of the country cannot, however, be described here.

After referring to the work of the missionary societies he thus gives expression to his opinion, "missionary efforts, however, will not avail to stop the slave trade, and open the country to civilisation, unless supplemented by commerce. Wherever commerce finds its way, there missionaries will follow, and wherever missionaries prove that white men can live and travel, there trade is certain to be established."

"The Portuguese," Cameron says, "hold the keys of the land route from Loanda and Benguelà, and keep out foreign capital and enterprise. If they threw open their ports; and encouraged the employment of capital, and the advent of energetic men of business, their provinces of Angola and Mozambique might rival the richest, and most prosperous of the dependencies of the British Crown. But a blind system of protection, carried on by underpaid officials, stifles trade; many of the Portuguese are aware of this, and lament it, but say, they are powerless."

The universal aptitude for trade, shown by the natives, is noticed by him.

A paper on "The Trade of Central Africa, Present and Future," was read by Commander Cameron before the African Committee of the Society of Arts on January 23, 1877. He says, "The rivers of this great continent are something marvellous. They are our great natural highways at present, but there are many parts of the continent which offer great facilities for constructing roads or tramways, or light lines of railway. The Zambesi, unfortunately, has its mouths in the possession of the Portuguese; I believe their government are acting for the best according to their lights, but their system of enormous protective duties, and of granting monopolies, and so on, has helped to stop the road to the interior by the Zambesi, and they are now attempting to annex the mouth of the Congo, and thus to practically seal up the waterways to the interior;" and it is stated in this paper, that " the people on Lake Nyassa are already finding that the duties charged by the Portuguese on the Zambesi, render it very unlikely that their work will be able to pay," and with reference to a road to Zanzibar it is said " if they could get a route to Zanzibar with only a small percentage of duty to the Sultan, it would have the effect of bringing down the high duties levied by the Portuguese on the Zambesi."

PART II.

Travellers who have recently visited the country confirm opinions previously maintained.

Lord Mayo, for instance, made a journey in 1882 through parts of Portuguese West Africa, traversing a distance of over 500 miles from Mossamedes to the river Cunéné. At the meeting of the Royal Geographical Society on June 11, 1883, he described his travels, and gave an interesting account of the productions, the vegetation, and the condition of the country. Sir H. Rawlinson, who occupied the chair, enquired what information could be given as to the nature and extent of the Portuguese authority, and Lord Mayo answered : " The duties are excessive, and in fact the Portuguese had completely ruined any chance of fair trade by the fearful duties which they imposed." The duties on some cotton goods, that Lord

Mayo took with him, were as much as one-third the invoiced price. It is stated that the keeper of the store at Humpata, 130 miles from the coast, in lat. 15° S., found it cheaper to drag his goods from Walvisch Bay, lat. 22° 52′ S. rather than to pay the excessive duties at Mossamedes. It is believed, however, that the Portuguese Government were going to make some effort to reduce the duties, and Lord Mayo says " if they did, they would greatly improve the country, as a more beautiful and fertile region could not well be imagined." In concluding the discussion, Sir H. Rawlinson remarked that " the observations of Lord Mayo were of considerable interest, not merely in reference to that particular part of Africa, but also to the great questions now being agitated on the Congo, where Portuguese jurisdiction and government, if established, might be supposed to be conducted very much on the same principles as farther south." He also said " it was interesting to know what were the relative positions in regard to the science of government of the International Exploration party, the French, and the Portuguese."

Major-General Sir F. J. Goldsmid visited the Congo last year, on behalf of the International Association, and in a descriptive paper read before the Royal Geographical Society on February 11, 1884, he said that the object of the Comité d'Études du Haut Congo was to determine the question of communications, and to enquire as to the establishment of commercial relations with the tribes, and the introduction of European manufactures in exchange for African products. A flag had been adopted and stations had been erected, but the motives of the Association were purely philanthropic, and he expressed a hope that the "free" stations of the Association would receive the support of the civilised world. Mr. Morgan, who accompanied General Goldsmid, described his journey to Stanley Pool. He says that whole regions have been depopulated by the slave trade, but observes that farther inland the population is more dense. The difficulties of the journey to

Stanley Pool appear from Mr. Morgan's account to be considerable ; a road, however, has been constructed. Mr. Morgan repeats the account we have heard from Mr. Stanley and Mr. Johnston, that 5000 miles of navigable rivers are accessible from Stanley Pool.

The difficulties that would beset philanthropists, missionaries, travellers, and merchants in gaining the navigable part of the river were remarked upon by Mr. Waller, and Mr. H. H. Johnston in reference to the so-called "*liberal terms*" at present in vogue in Mozambique, said, "those who knew anything of Mozambique would think that the terms were rather *illiberal* than otherwise. He, therefore, thought it a very unfortunate thing if Portugal was allowed to occupy Landana and Banana (at the mouth of the Congo), the two points which would affect the Congo in the future." It is important to put this opinion of Mr. Johnston clearly forward, for he has been supposed to be an advocate, or at least an apologist, for the treaty. We shall refer to his views again.

General Sir F. Goldsmid stated at the same meeting, that he thought there was now scarcely any trace whatever of Portuguese dominion in those parts (the Congo region); at the present day he did not suppose that the Portuguese were better known along the river banks than the English, Dutch, French, or other nations there represented. At Loanda, of course, Portuguese influence prevailed, as also farther down the coast for some distance ; but it was generally understood that a 'white' man could not go from Loanda to Ambritz without being molested by the natives. He said, "a statement to this effect will be found in Mr. Monteiro's clever book on Angola, published about nine years ago, and he (Sir Frederic) had learnt on trustworthy local authority, corroborated, to the best of his recollection, by a Portuguese gentleman, on board the steamer, on which he travelled, that such was, still, the case."

With regard to the trade on the Upper Congo, General Goldsmid did not think that as yet there had been any palpable increase in the imports and exports, but this result could hardly be expected so soon. He had little doubt, that when more stations had been formed, and the aims and objects of the Association were more clearly understood, the whole would in time become centres, as it were, of traffic, and a great impetus would be given to commerce and the march of civilisation.

The President (Lord Aberdare) in the course of his remarks said, that he would not be tempted by the political hints that had been thrown out, to enter into the question whether or not Mr. Gladstone was going to violate his promise, that the treaty with Portugal should be submitted to the House of Commons, nor whether the Dutch merchants had received information as to the contents of the treaty, which were not known in this country. He had no doubt, that in process of time it would be found that Her Majesty's Government would do all that they had promised to do, and submit their treaty to the consideration of Parliament; and he was bound to say that if they had shown too great consideration for the interests of Portugal, it could not be for want of ample notice, in Parliament and out, of the opinion of the mercantile community of this country. The President concluded by observing that such considerations were not for their society. Their interests were geographical, and the progress of geography led to commerce.

If we are not referring at too great length to the proceedings of the Geographical Society, a paper by Mr. Johnston should be mentioned. He tells us that the country between Loanda and Ambritz, "although nominally owned by the Portuguese, is almost impassable for a European, owing to the animosity of the natives." Mr. Johnston, it must be remembered, is one of our most recent travellers. In the interior, some ten miles from "independent, cosmopolitan Kinsembo," he says, "the landscapes are so many earthly paradises, with their massive groves, and verdant slopes and prosperous plantations. About a mile from the coast near Ambrizette, the scenery is beautiful and park-like." He says "the natives of Ambrizette are decidedly opposed to any idea of future annexation or protection by a European power." The fine harbour which would pass to Portugal under the treaty is then described. "At the mouth of the Congo, on the inner side of the little promontory of Banana, there is a deep and capacious inlet of the Congo, where there is room for a whole navy to be moored. Here, ships of the greatest size, can be anchored within fifty yards of the shore."

The commercial and political side of the question is not treated in Mr. Johnston's interesting book on the Congo, which contains such graphic descriptions of the scenery and natural history of the country; reference on this head must be made to his paper on the "Portuguese Colonies in West Africa," read before the Society of Arts on the 12th of February, 1884.

"Since I left West Africa," he says, "the Portuguese have formally taken possession of a point on the south-west coast a little to the north of the Congo. This is generally called Landana, and is situated close to the embouchure of the river Chiloango, an important highway into the interior. Landana is nearly 100 miles from the mouth of the Congo, but receives a great deal of the Congo trade, which follows the course of the Chiloango."

It may here be mentioned that the Under Secretary for Foreign Affairs, on the 23rd of April, 1883, in reply to Mr. Jacob Bright, stated that "orders have been issued to the Governor of Angola not to occupy an inch of territory in dispute during the progress of negotiations, but to maintain strictly the *status quo*."

Ambritz, to which further reference will be made, is described by Mr. Johnston as the "natural" outlet for the trade of all the interior lying about the 7th and 8th degrees of south latitude, and stretching inland to the river Luango; but he is obliged to add, "it does not seem to prosper somehow, in spite of being the only kind of port between Loanda and the Congo.

Many of its merchants have migrated across the Portuguese boundary to Kinsembo, where, perhaps, the landing is the most dangerous on all the south-west coast, in order to escape the duties imposed by the Portuguese custom-house." The traveller then turns attention to a district a little farther to the south. "The intervening district between the river Dande (spelt Dante in the narrative of the Capuchin missionaries who left Italy on a mission to the Congo in 1666) and Ambritz has never been conquered by the Portuguese, and still remains impassable to Europeans. A force of twenty armed policemen would suffice to clear the road, but, although Portugal can dream of military expeditions to the Congo, she cannot afford a few soldiers to connect Loanda with Ambritz by land."

Alluding to the extent of the Portuguese African possessions, Mr. Johnston estimates that as much as 1,000,000 square miles of African Continent is now under the rule and administration of Portugal. After some observations (and the hospitality the Portuguese invariably show to travellers must be acknowledged), intended to place the Portuguese system in as fair a light as possible, Mr. Johnston says by way of qualification that he does not intend to advance "a plea for an extension of Portuguese power over fresh parts of Africa." He proceeds, indeed, to say that "Portugal has sufficient colonies at the present day to last her all her political lifetime; and yet, while she pleads poverty as an excuse for not developing what she has already got, she can afford to equip costly expeditions in view of farther and fantastic conquests. The idea of Portugal on the Congo is simply preposterous." Mr. Johnston concludes by saying "The more one travels in Africa, the more one arrives at the conclusion that the Portuguese have got the pick of the coast lands; but, unfortunately, another conviction forces itself on the mind, that they have more than they can be reasonably expected to develop with their individual resources."

We now turn to another authority, Mr. Capper, Lloyd's agent for the Congo district, who read a paper on the Congo and the Niger, before the Society of Arts (reported in the Journal for the 11th of April, 1884). It has been said, in some quarters, that the Congo trade is insignificant; Mr. Capper, however, states that " the imports and exports of the West African trade have risen from 28,000, tons in 1868, to 200,000 in 1882, and steamers are now constantly running between England and the Congo, and the Niger;" and he gives his opinion that " as long as these rivers are free, legitimate commerce will thrive apace." Mr. Capper speaks with personal knowledge and experience, having resided in West Africa for seven years, and having traded on both these rivers. He say; " The commerce of the Congo is of recent growth. In my time, twelve years ago, there were four English houses, one French, and one Dutch, trading up the river as far as Nokki, there are now forty-nine European factories on the banks, and the exports and imports are valued at £2,000,000." " The Niger and the Congo," he asserts, " are the present entrances to Africa, and if England is true to its trust, it will not let them be recklessly thrown away."

On this question of the extent of the Congo trade the statement of the Chairman of the Manchester Chamber of Commerce should be noticed. He estimated the exports alone of British goods to the territory from 5° 12′ to 8° S. latitude a few years ago at £500,000 per annum, now at £1,000,000, and the exports and imports together at £2,000,000. Sir J. Lee considers this an over-estimate; but granting that it is so, does Sir J. Lee take into account that the effect of the treaty would be, not to increase the trade, but certainly to curtail it?

In the discussion upon Mr. Capper's paper, Mr. Tomlinson, M.P. for Preston, adverted to " the importance of opening up Africa to commerce, as the trade of this country was suffering from the very want which Africa was capable of supplying,* viz., a market for our goods, and the question was whether the

* See note 1, page 44.

command of the West African market should be given to a nation which was not, as England was, a commercial nation. The Portuguese had no manufacture and no commerce of the kind required for the African market." Alluding to the application of the Mozambique tariff, he drew special attention to the effect the imposition of 10 per cent. would have "*on the introduction of British goods*" to the African market.*

To refer again to the Congo trade, a letter dated Ponta da Lenha, December 30, has been reprinted from the *Manchester Examiner* of March 13th, and it is stated by the writer that "the oppressive duties imposed by Portugal on the province of Angola have driven into the Congo many European traders. Portuguese traders have also found it next to impossible to transact business subject to the extortion of the officials. Hence, they, too, have sought refuge on the Congo River, and they do not care to be followed by the system from which they believed they had escaped." He also says that the trade with the natives has now "become very considerable," and the claim of Portugal is asserted to the detriment both of natives and Europeans. He proceeds, "Do not be misled by the fallacy that trade exists on the Congo, and that ours is of no importance;" and adds, "What increase there has been is here in the Lower Congo, and here if we have fair play, such as we have a right to demand from our countrymen, the centre of commerce must necessarily continue."

This is a sufficient answer to Lord Fife's allusion in the House of Lords on April 24th, 1884, to the "little" amount of trade on the Congo. He did say, however, that, at present, the Lower Congo possesses what trade there is.

* See note 2, page 44.

PART III.

Another point must be now considered. How far is the Congo navigable ? With reference to the Lower Congo, General Goldsmid says in a letter to the *Times*, in reply to Mr. Johnston, that "nothing but the merest cockleshell propelled by steam can pass up between Nokki and Vivi, and that up to Nokki but few seagoing craft ever venture."

This is important, as a great deal is said about free transit being secured by treaty stipulation.

The great waterway into Central Africa by the river Congo only commences, so to speak, at Stanley Pool, the river as a means of communication with the interior being the object of our consideration. The question, therefore, is by what route, and by what methods, can Stanley Pool be reached. There is some distance to be traversed, and a connecting link is required in the chain of communications. Until further surveys of the country have been taken, and more accurate knowledge is acquired, no opinion (keeping the cost of transport in view) can really be given as to the route, and the best means for carrying goods overland from the deep waters in the estuary of the Congo to Stanley Pool. Whether starting from Boma, the rugged and hilly ground should be followed, using the road made by the International Association under the direction of Mr. Stanley, and making available a portion of the river between the falls ; or whether another route (always considering the cost of transport) is to be taken, is as yet uncertain. It can only be determined by further enquiry.

Lord Fife, when asking his question on the 24th of April in the House of Lords, after observing that " the Lower Congo led practically nowhere," said that " the recent labours of Mr. Stanley and Mr. Johnston abundantly proved that the best route in the future by which to reach Central Africa was the Kwilu river." In regard to this, a point may, no doubt, be made by advocates in search of arguments on behalf of the treaty. The results of recent expeditions go to prove, it is said, that the Kwilu is practicable for some distance as a means of entering the country, and that a possible route for a line of railway may be found by following the course of the river, and then working across the country to Stanley Pool. The Kwilu is outside the territory that would pass to Portugal under the treaty. An attempt, it seems, is being made to diminish the importance of the Lower Congo trade, and at the same time it is asserted that the route to the great artery of the upper river is still left free to all the world.

Mr. Capper has had considerable experience in railway works, and he has been a trader in West Africa. He was asked a question at the recent meeting of the Society of Arts as to a possible railway route to Stanley Pool, and with reference to the Kwilu river, and he thus replied : " As to the Kwilu river, from a commercial point of view, it did not do for people to go to new rivers and commence laying down railways. What a man of commerce liked was that his commerce should grow as he put his hands in his pocket. The principal part of the trade of the Congo came from the southern bank, and, as the Kwilu was some distance to the north, the whole of the trade would have to cross the river; there would be the same difficulties as at the Falls of Yellala ; there must be land carriage of some kind. It was due to British enterprise alone that matters of that kind had been already dealt with in Africa."

The existing circumstances and condition of the country, and the necessities of trade, must be taken into consideration. A correspondent writing from Ponta da Lenha in the *Pall Mall Gazette* thus gives his opinion : " Improved means of communication can only be serviceable where it is sufficiently cheap to be profitable to those using it," and this writer seem to question the utility for commercial purposes of the road constructed to Stanley Pool, on account of the expense of transport.

Mr. Bentley, a missionary, who has spent five years on the

Congo, gives his views in the *Pall Mall Gazette* for May 20th, in this journal's Topics of the Day. Speaking of Mr. Johnston, he says, " Many of his leading positions are fundamentally unsound. Take, for instance, his point that the true entrance to the Upper Congo is by the Kwilu, not by the Lower Congo. Now, not a single ocean steamer can go up that river, which is only partly navigable by boats of small burden. It takes you nearly 200 miles out of your right course, it traverses a country peopled by natives very hostile to trade, and the tract across which Mr. Johnston would place his railway—from Stéphanie-ville to one of the tributaries of Stanley Pool—is a region across which I was assured by a Belgian representative of the International African Association it would be difficult, not to say impossible, to construct a line of railway. The true entrance to the Upper Congo is a port opposite Ponta da Lenha, on the southern bank. From this point, where ocean steamers can discharge in safety, there would be comparatively small engineering difficulties in constructing a line passing through the Bas-Congo country to Léopoldville. By this means the cargoes destined for the Upper Congo would pass direct from the ship that brought them from Liverpool or London to the railway, which would have its terminus on the Upper Congo, and from thence goods might be despatched in river boats throughout the whole interior of Africa." " The line," said Mr. Bentley, " would pass through a country presenting few engineering difficulties. For the most part fairly level, and traversing through the whole of its route tribes well disposed to Europeans and keenly attached to trade, there is everything in its favour."

Would it not be our best and most prudent course, with the view, alone, of improving the means (that may be undertaken some day—perhaps before long), of approaching from the coast this great inland waterway of the Upper Congo, to leave the Lower Congo and all the adjoining territory, as free as possible from restrictions of any kind ? Shall we not thus be really aiding the opening up of vast fertile, densely-populated regions to commerce? One of the existing trade routes, it should be added, now follows a line from Stanley Pool to Ambrizette, and Ambrizette would under the treaty, fall within the rule of Portugal.

Next, with regard to France: In his speech in Parliament last year Mr. Jacob Bright said: "There is an opinion, I do not know how far it is well founded—that what has been done and said by a subject of France (M. De Brazza) in Africa has somewhat disturbed people's minds, and has had some influence at the Foreign Office. Some of those who have communicated with me think that there has been a great exaggeration in regard to this matter, and that it may only result in a salutary extension of French commerce."

In the Journal of the Royal Geographical Society for August, 1883, in page 483, it is stated that the news from the headquarters of the International Association at Brussels is to the effect that Mr. Stanley has stringent orders to maintain a friendly understanding with the French Expedition, and to show deference to the rights acquired by France on the Congo. At the Geographical Society's meeting on February 11, 1884, Commander Cameron spoke in high terms of M. De Brazza. A more modest man, he said, could not be found. He was an enthusiast in his work, and Cameron added that he did not think any Englishman would set that down as a failing.

As to the opinion entertained by the French Government, Mr. W. E. Forster, in *The Times* of April the 14th, draws attention to a despatch of Lord Granville's of the 1st of June, 1883, in which our Foreign Minister says: "M. Challemel Lacour, in a recent conversation with her Majesty's ambassador at Paris, distinctly denied that the pretensions of Portugal to that part of the coast (the Lower Congo district) are admitted by France."

As regards Holland, a Reuter's telegram, in *The Morning Post* of April the 28th, reports that the Dutch minister for Foreign Affairs stated in the First Chamber of the States General that the commercial interests of the Netherlands gave the Government the right to defend the same, as, in fact, it had already done, and he added : " Holland does not demand any rights of sovereignty, but demands simply to protect her commercial interests, which are ignored by the treaty which has been concluded. The Government reserves to itself liberty of action, and is prepared to accept the responsibility of its decision."

The following appears in the *Times* of May the 16th, with reference to the views held by Germany :

BERLIN, *May* 15.

Prince Bismarck has sent the following answer to the Chamber of Commerce of Frankfort-on-the-Maine, as well as to the several other bodies of a similar kind which had sent in remonstrances to the Foreign Office on the subject of the Anglo-Portuguese treaty :—

" BERLIN, *May* 12, 1884.

" In reply to your favour of the 8th inst. with reference to the Congo Treaty concluded between England and Portugal, I beg to state that I regard as justifiable the objections raised by the organs to German commerce to the stipulations of the treaty affecting German trade. To this view I have given expression to both the said Governments, notifying, at the same time, to them that the Government of His Majesty the Emperor would never be able to admit the applicability of these stipulations to the subjects of the Empire. At present we are engaged in an exchange of opinion on this question with the Governments of the countries most concerned in the trade with Africa, and I hope that this exchange of opinion will lead to a settlement of commercial relations in the Congo territory, which also takes German interests into account.

" VON BISMARCK."

Mr. Johnston having stated in a letter to the *Times* that there were only two alternatives, and that it was a question of either France or Portugal on the Lower Congo, General Sir F.

Goldsmid wrote in reply, pointing out that the choice was not so limited as Mr. Johnston believed, and that Holland might with equal propriety have been suggested, and he observed that Mr. Johnston omitted " the by no means unimportant, if abandoned, alternative of an International Commission." Lord Granville, we know, did not succeed in prevailing upon the Portuguese Government to acquiesce in the suggestion of an International Commission. Mr. Johnston seems also to have ignored (we shall not perhaps be far wrong in using the expression), the " desire " of the Congo traders to be left alone. It should not be forgotten by whose capital and enterprise the trade of the Congo district has been created.

As to the position on the Congo of the International Association, to which so much attention is now being given, some further allusion may here be made, though an enquiry into the objects and work of the Association is beyond the scope of this paper.

The *Times*, of April 24, contained a telegram, announcing that the American Senate has concurred in the President's recommendation to recognise the International Association.

Replying to Lord Fife's question in the House of Lords on April 24, as to whether the Government intended to recognise the Association, Lord Granville said " the noble earl had referred to a very large, important, and difficult matter, in regard to which he was not prepared to give a definite answer on the present occasion. He understood that the Association referred to in the question of the noble earl was promoted by the King of the Belgians, not as a Sovereign, but as an individual who had carried out the scheme on philanthropic grounds with immense munificence. The Association was not separated, he thought, from commercial objects, and under the energetic conduct of its leader, Mr. Stanley, very large and important results had been achieved. With regard to the recognition of the society by Her Majesty's Government, he might say that the noble earl had correctly referred to the recognition of it by the Government of the United States. He had himself to-day received a telegram showing that the Government of the Unite 1 States had recognised the flag of the Association as that of a friendly government. The whole question of the constitution of the society was, of course, very important. Her Majesty's Government had not, under consideration, at present, the particular question which the noble earl had put, and they would have to go much farther into detail as to the matter and the view which was held by the Government of the United States before giving any definite answer to the question."

The writer of the letter in the *Pall Mall Gazette*, from Ponta da Lenha, already referred to, is not complimentary to the Association, but the tone (if it does express the view of the Lower Congo traders) may, perhaps, be accounted for on the ground of a belief, that but for the existence of the Association, there might have been one pretext less for a treaty injurious to trade.

The Association by carrying on still further the work of the pioneer, undertaking scientific surveys, and making roads and communications, will be giving an impetus and encouragement to the opening of trade with this part of Africa. This, indeed, seems to be its very *raison d'etre*. Its philanthropic leaders devote their resources to such purposes. In the course of their work, and in establishing outlying stations, which have been carried far up the river into the interior of Africa, they have proved that Europeans can live in the country. If by the efforts of the Association, and the enterprise of individuals, trade can in the future be developed with these regions, it ought to be the object of our Government to see that the commerce of all nations is equally entitled to benefit.

One more allusion to engineering and other works. Mr. Capper's advice should be kept in view. The cost of transport is to be regarded, whether it is by the Association or by some other agency that works are undertaken. Trade should be en ourage l. The producer must see his profit. The African in these regions, it must be remembered, has a tendency to be contented with gathering the abundant fruits of the earth, without labour; he must be taught and "induced" to cultivate the soil.

In the *National Review* for May, General Goldsmi l thus concludes an article on "Portugal and the Congo." "We have spoken of the International African Association: the American Senate recognise this as the chief po ver on the Congo. Possessor of an extensive territory in the region of the river, the history of its rapid rise is too well known that we should here attempt to recount it. . . . But we may say from personal knowledge of locality and *personnel*, that its disinterested objects are as manifest to the minds of disinterested people as are its steamers and stations to the eye of the ordinary traveller. And we woul l ask whether it is not time that this outcome of royal generosity, and munificent philanthropy should be acknowledged by Europe at large, and have the *status* of a distinct colonial power? Had such ackn wledgment been made a year ago, it is probable that the guardianship of the Lower Congo would have been disposed of, so far as England is concerned, in a way less provocative of criticism than in the case of the transfer to Portugal."

The *Times* of May 16 contains the following intelligence:—

"BRUSSELS, *May* 15.

"An Antwerp journal states that the International African Association is elaborating its Constitution as a free Federal State established on the Congo.

"The same journal affirms positively that an agreement has been concluded between France and the Association, the documents bearing the signatures of M. Ferry for France, and of Colonel Strauch for the Association."

The particulars that the *Times* of May 20th gives of this agreement will be read with interest: "We understand that the following are the terms of the arrangement which has been concluded between the Government of the French Republic and the Association Internationale du Congo :—France pledges herself to respect the stations and the free territories of the Association, as also to recognise the exercise by the Association of the rights which it has acquired. The Association undertakes not to dispose of its possessions, but in the event of circumstances compelling their abandonment, the option of purchasing is reserved in the first instance to the French Government. The agreement whereby the United States Government recognises the flag of the Association Internationale, already provides that no customs duties are to be levied on goods imported into the territories of the Association, and that equal rights as regards residence, dealings in land, and general trading privileges, are to be accorded to the citizens of every nationality."

PART IV.

The manner in which the attempts that have been made on the part of the Portuguese Government to acquire an extension of territory on the West African coast from latitude 5° 12' to 8° have been met by Great Britain, shall now be shown.

A passage from a paper read before the Society of Arts will be quoted here, as it will lead us to a consideration of this branch of the subject. On the 16th of March, 1877, Mr. Irvine thus described to the Society the results of the Portuguese occupation of Ambritz. " The Portuguese," he said, " immediately established a custom-house under a full fig of officials. On the opposite side of the river stands another trading station, known as Kinsembo, from which, before the occupation of Ambritz by the Portuguese, large quantities of copper ore were exported, thirty to fifty tons being a common ballast for a vessel ; but since the arrival of the Portuguese on the opposite shore the trade has absolutely died out, and whenever you ask the natives the reason of this, they tell you quite openly that if they showed you the riches of their country the Portuguese would come and take possession of it. Within the last few months " (the paper is dated 16th March, 1877) " the Portuguese have actually laid claim to this very place (Kinsembo), to Ambrizette, to Banana, and up to the Congo, the Congo itself included, but on representations being made to Her Majesty's Government, such decided steps were taken by Lord Derby that by last mail instructions went out from the Government at Lisbon to the Governor of Angola to withdraw absolutely from any attempt to extend their territory beyond what is now recognised as theirs, in virtue of actual occupation."

With the view of placing in a clear light the manner in which the claims of Portugal have been always regarded, some points in the correspondence published in the African Parliamentary Papers must here be touched upon.

Lord Palmerston, in his despatch of September 26, 1846, to Lord Howard de Walden, referring to " territories over which His most faithful Majesty has declared that he maintains his rights," says that " while the right of Portugal to exclusive sovereignty, and jurisdiction from 8° to 18° S. latitude, was fully recognised by the British Government, her right over territory from 5° 12′ down to 8° was not so recognised." Allusion is made to an apprehension expressed by the Loanda Court lest an enforcement by Portugal of sovereign rights over the territory from 5° 12′ to 8°, " would much interfere with the intercourse of British merchants with the natives, who at present carry on their trade, which must be an increasing one, without the payment of any dues to the Portuguese Government." " To pass without notice a sentence of the Portuguese Court which involves a claim of exclusive territorial possession," Lord Palmerston observes, " might prejudice the right which it is important *in the interests of commerce* for Her Majesty's

Government to maintain to unrestricted intercourse with that part of the west coast of Africa, which lies between 5°, 12', and 8°."

Lord Palmerston's solicitude for the " interests of commerce " should be noticed ; and it becomes important to lay stress on this declaration of Lord Palmerston's, as in the statements made by Her Majesty's present Government it is not made to appear that the " interests of commerce " did form a ground for Lord Palmerston's resistance to the claims of Portugal. Another inference, in fact, might be drawn from the letter Lord Granville wrote on March 21st to the Chairman of the Manchester Chamber of Commerce in vindication of the treaty, in which he says: " A policy which was formerly justifiable for the prevention of the slave trade may have ceased to be so, under the altered circumstances of a time when the slave trade on the West Coast has ceased to exist.'

Again, writing to Baron Moncorvo, on November 30th, 1846, Lord Palmerston speaks of the right which it is important "*in the interests of commerce,* for Her Majesty's Government to maintain to unrestricted intercourse with this territory."

In similar terms, Lord Clarendon, in his despatch of November 26, 1853, repeats "the declaration of Her Majesty's Government that the *interests of commerce* render it imperative upon them to maintain the right to unrestrained intercourse with that part of the west coast of Africa which lies between 5°, 12', and 8° S. latitude."

When it was announced in 1855 that an armed force would be sent to Molemba, Lord Clarendon, in his despatch of April 6, said " it would be the duty of Her Majesty's Government to oppose " such a determination of the Portuguese Government ; and it should be noticed that Lord Clarendon added that " Foreign nations would thus " (if Portugal carried out its object) " be debarred from having free intercourse with the place."

The occupation of Ambritz was effected in 1855. The effect of the occupation was most injurious to the interests of commerce, though it might have been very different if the promise made by the Portuguese had really been fulfilled, and if they had acted according to their word, viz., "that they did not intend to make any alteration with regard to commercial intercourse with that place, nor to impose any duties." See Mr. Ward's Despatch to Lord Clarendon, August 8th, 1855.

Having succeeded at Ambritz, the Portuguese Government were attempting to treat the territories of Cabinda and Molemba, north of the Congo, as included in the province of Angola, and with reference to this, Lord Clarendon says in his despatch of August 15th, 1856, that "any attempt at territorial extension will be resisted by force."

With reference to Kinsembo (which would pass under the present treaty to Portugal), Lord Russell wrote in his despatch to Count Lavradio on the 28th of July, 1860, "I cannot omit to notice at once the statement in your letter of the 9th inst., that Kinsembo appertains to the Crown of Portugal. You must be aware that Her Majesty's Government have invariably resisted this claim." Lord Russell informs Count Lavradio that "although Her Majesty's Government acquiesced in the occupation of Ambritz, any attempt to extend that occupation to other parts of the coast would be opposed by Her Majesty's naval forces."

No stronger language could be used than is to be found in Lord Russell's despatch of the 13th of October, 1860, when he informs Count Lavradio that "the interests of Portugal would be far better consulted by developing the resources of the vast territories which she already possesses in Africa, than by seeking to extend a barren sovereignty over farther tracts of country on that continent, which can only be acquired by violence and bloodshed."

In 1867 Lord Derby (then Lord Stanley) wrote on the 21st of August to Mr. Harris: "With regard to the claim now again put forward on behalf of the Portuguese Crown to the sovereignty of the territory lying between 5° 12' and 8°, it will be right that you should ask for some explanation from the Government of His Faithful Majesty, because if no notice is taken of this claim, it may lead to serious differences between the British and Portuguese naval forces on the West African station, as the instructions which were issued in 1856 to the British naval commanders to prevent the occupation by the Portuguese of the territory in question still hold good, and will be acted upon if necessary."

A different attitude having been adopted by the present Government throughout the negotiations that they have carried on with the Government of Portugal, it is necessary to hear any explanation that can be given as to their views and objects.

For this purpose we have to look to the speech in Parliament of the Under Secretary for Foreign Affairs, during the debate last year on the motion of Mr. Jacob Bright; and we must ask our readers to give their attention seriously to the question of the sufficiency of the reasons, and of the adequacy of the pleas that have been advanced on behalf of the Government.

The Under Secretary for Foreign Affairs said that he considered Mr. Bright's speech an indictment of the policy of the Government, and he had, therefore, he says " to show the reasons which had induced the Government to depart, up to a certain point, from the attitude hitherto observed by the Foreign Office in regard to this question." He observed that he would not altogether admit that Her Majesty's Government had departed from the attitude taken upon this question by the eminent statesmen alluded to by Mr. Whitley, viz., Lord Clarendon, Lord Russell, Lord Palmerston, and the present Lord Derby, and he asserted that the attitude taken by them—"that they did not recognise the position of the Portuguese in this region, was still the attitude of Her Majesty's Government." Lord E. Fitzmaurice then proceeded to say that " Her Majesty's Government considered that circumstances had since arisen, which, they believed, had they arisen in former days, would have induced the Government to consider, whether they did not furnish adequate reasons for taking, up to a certain point, a new departure."

This, it must be confessed, seems rather a subtle distinction between what is, and what is not a "new departure."

The fact is plain and simple, that Lord Granville by his despatch of the 15th of March, 1883, admits that "the claim of Portugal is not established." The Government does not recognise the validity of an old claim to territory between latitudes 5° 12' and 8° S. "over which *Portugal has not had any right.*"

It is, however, equally plain that by the first article of the treaty "Her Britannic Majesty *agrees to recognise the sovereignty* of His Most Faithful Majesty the King of Portugal and the Algaves over that part of the West Coast of Africa situated between 8° and 5°·12' S. latitude."

This most important point as to sovereignty is the turning-point of the whole question. It is the foundation on which the treaty rests. The Government agree to allow the exercise of the Portuguese jurisdiction over the territory claimed. A total change of position. It is altogether a "new departure," and a reversal of the policy of the predecessors in office of Her Majesty's Government. It is this, the bringing in of the sovereign jurisdiction of Portugal to the hitherto free territory, and not whether, the validity of the claim has been admitted as of right or not, that is of vital moment to the traders, and the vast commercial interests concerned. No wonder that this has been called not merely a concession, but a "surrender."

Lord E. Fitzmaurice having observed that "it was difficult to say at what exact moment the present stage of the negotiations began," it will be well to bear in mind the date of the affair at the mouth of the Congo, reported by Mr. Hopkins in his despatch of the 28th of April, 1877, as having then lately occurred. The previous year, on the 8th of February, Lord Derby at the time Her Majesty's Secretary of State for Foreign Affairs had written a despatch to the Duke of Saldanha, apparently disposing in the clearest manner of the Portuguese claims, and expressing "the earnest hope of Her Majesty's Government that the Government of Lisbon will issue no instructions to their authorities on the West Coast of Africa, which will alter the existing state of things on that coast, inasmuch as the orders which were issued in 1856 to the commander of Her Majesty's cruisers to oppose any attempt on the part of the Portuguese authorities to extend the dominions of Portugal north of Ambritz, and of which the Portuguese Government were informed at the time remain still in force." The affair at the mouth of the Congo, occurred, as we have said, early in 1877. Sir J. Pauncefoot, on the 21st of August, 1877, wrote from the Foreign Office to Mr. Consul Hopkins, with reference to the case of Scott (one of the persons concerned in the affair on the Congo), stating in this despatch that Her Majesty's Government "have always contested and opposed " the claims to the territory made by the Portuguese Government."

There is no wavering here, no deviation from the position always maintained towards the claims of Portugal, nor is there the least loophole afforded, or encouragement given for treating the affair at the mouth of the Congo as a pretext.

It is clear, then, that up to 1877 the claims of Portugal were firmly resisted; and the Portuguese Government had failed to acquire jurisdiction, or gain any foothold in the territory in question.

There is no other despatch published until we come to the year 1882. The chairman of the Manchester Chamber of Commerce in his speech to the Chamber on March the 17th, 1884, drew notice to the fact that "there is no record published of any importunity on the part of Portugal to get anything from the year 1877 to 1882."

The commercial progress of the free territories had gone on increasing through the enterprise of traders of various nations, not especially Portuguese (the exact proportion of purely Portuguese factories, is not yet, it seems quite accurately ascertained). That it would gratify the pride and ambition of

the Portuguese to see these territories included in the possessions of the Crown of Portugal is easy to understand. The
desire of the Portuguese Government to place them under
similar fiscal, and other regulations to those of the Portuguese
African possessions is natural enough.*

PART V.

The claims of Portugal are again advanced in 1882. Senhor
Serpa, in his lengthy despatch of the 8th of November, renews
the demands of Portugal on various grounds, and alludes, among
other matters, to the affair on the Congo in 1877.

Whatever the Portuguese point of view may be, our wish is
to discover the ground for the " new departure" on the part of
Her Majesty's Government, and to ascertain the " new circumstances" that have " arisen" to justify the change of policy.

The objects of the Government, are explained in Lord Granville's Letter from the Foreign Office on March 21st, addressed
to the chairman of the Manchester Chamber of Commerce.
The letter, published in *The Times*, attracts attention. Lord
Granville states that he " thinks that on further consideration
the Chamber may see reason to modify the views expressed"
in their communication of March 6th in opposition to the
treaty, and he speaks of " disputes, which in the absence of
treaty engagements may lead to local bloodshed, and ultimately to even more serious consequences;" and observes, " I
would call your attention to the fact that only within the last
few weeks serious disputes between the natives and traders
have arisen at Nokki and at Moculla, and that at the latter
place forty natives were killed by the fire of the Dutch traders
from their fort, and that ultimately the Portuguese were called
in to keep the peace, through the action of the traders them-

* See notes 3 and 4, page 45.

selves, including the local representative of at least one important British firm."

Mr. Jacob Bright in his speech last year dealt with the question of order and security in the Congo district. He said : " As to the general security of the country merchants make no complaint. They pay an annual tribute, and there the matter ends. The missionaries make no complaint. Nobody in that region complains. I have looked at the official papers, presented to the House a few days ago, containing a correspondence between Her Majesty's Government and that of Portugal from the year 1845 to the year 1877. During this period *there is no evidence of disorder* until the year 1877."

The chairman of the Manchester Chamber of Commerce, Mr. Hutton, stated in his speech before the Chamber that " it is because the trade is free, because there is a peaceful way of conducting it, because no difficulty is met with in trading with the natives that the trade has gone on extending," and again, " not only is the trade free, but it is *very rarely that the peace of the trade is disturbed.* I will challenge any one to show an instance during the last thirty or forty years where that trade has hitherto been disturbed to any serious extent." Mr. Hutton further says, " The British Government saw the importance of this free trade thirty or forty years ago, and we have in the book I hold in my hand eleven treaties with the chiefs and headmen of this district for securing the peaceful carrying on of this trade." " These treaties, from which I have quoted, were signed by the chiefs of their own will; they were not wrung from them." It may be mentioned that a letter was published in the *Morning Post* on April 19th, from "A Ten Years' Resident on the Coast," who states that "the agents have always lived on the most friendly terms with the natives;" and with regard to the affair alluded to by Lord Granville as having occurred at Nokki and Moculla, the correspondent of the *Morning Post* says : " This affair took place at Muculla (on the coast), a long, long way from Nokki, last year, and is a veritable instance of how old sores will at times be raked up, to make capital of. There were under thirty natives killed, and it was through the unfortunate explosion of a powder store, otherwise very likely not one man would have lost his life. The natives here had hitherto performed the work of labourers at the Dutch factory, and the agent having employed some Kroomen to do this, the natives of the place looked upon the innovation as an infringement of their rights. As the agent would not send the Kroomen away the natives attacked the factory. This shows conclusively that the natives are free and independent. Had the natives submitted this dispute to a 'palaver,' as is invariably the case, it would have been settled with advantage to both parties." And it may be observed that it has been stated in the *Manchester Courier* with reference to the recent disturbances, that " no doubt seems to exist on the coast that Portuguese political instigation was the cause of them. Supposing, however, that the attacks of the natives were made spontaneously, the assistance afforded by the Portuguese authorities is altogether misrepresented. Should a settlement, no matter to which nation it belongs, be attacked, all the white people assist in its defence. If a Portuguese man-of-war be in the neighbourhood, help is naturally asked for, but just the same assistance is asked of any vessel near, of whatever nationality, whether French, English, or Dutch."

To this affair at Moculla, and to the occurrence on the Congo in 1877, too great importance and prominence may easily be accorded. The Portuguese have their own claims to establish, and arguments brought forward by the Portuguese Government in a diplomatic correspondence require sifting before they can, at once, be admitted. Her Majesty's Government seem almost to be adopting and emphasising the Portuguese line of argument.

It would appear to be more in accordance with the facts, taking the whole of the circumstances together, to regard these occurrences as exceptional and isolated cases; for, throughout the narratives and recorded experiences of residents, traders, and missionaries, the condition of the district is represented as on the whole free from disturbance. The generally prevailing state of affairs both as between the traders themselves, and as between the traders and natives, is orderly and peaceful.

The Government propose that Great Britain should enter into the present treaty for the reasons explained by Lord Granville in his letter. "Speaking generally," he says, "the treaty has been entered into to establish security and peace on the Congo." How far the necessity exists, for the preservation of order, for calling in a European Power, and the Portuguese Government in particular, is for our Government to explain.

In a somewhat different sense to that contemplated by Lord Granville when writing his letter of March 21st, 1884, protection and assistance for the peaceful conduct of trade may, indeed, become necessary. Landana, at the mouth of the Chiloango, was last year, it seems, for a time at all events, occupied by the Portuguese. A question in Parliament, on March 8th, 1883, was asked by Baron de Worms, and the Under Secretary for Foreign Affairs replied "that the Portuguese Minister had informed him that no force was being prepared, and that while negotiations were pending no ships would be dispatched to the West Coast." Again, on March 19th, in reply to Baron de Worms, the Under Secretary stated that "the Portuguese Minister had recently repeated the assurance that no naval expedition would be sent to the Congo pending negotiations."

On the general question of the preservation of order and security in African territories, it should be remembered that the influence exercised by the British Consul at Zanzibar is a most beneficial one. It is felt, we are told, not only along the coast near Zanzibar, but far and wide into Central Africa. Then, in Central Africa, in the neighbourhood of the great Lakes, a British Consul is established. On the West side of Africa, can no means be found for enabling traders on the Congo to have the protection of a British Consul? The British Consul might be in easy communication, whenever needed, with British ships of war; or at least a couple of gunboats at the call of the British Consul might supply all that is necessary for the preservation of order and security in the district of the Congo. The calling in of Portuguese authorities might not, under such circumstances, be needed.

Mr. Jacob Bright expressed, in his speech, the opinion that "if an authority is established there (on the Congo) which does not now exist, it should be one in which the natives can have confidence and which the traders can respect;" adding that "if a change is made it should be a change for the better."

PART VI.

With regard to the great question of slavery, it is said by Lord Granville, in his letter in justification of the treaty, that it "contains valuable stipulations in regard to the abolition of slavery," the expression used in the treaty itself is "to provide for the complete extinction of the slave trade."

It is by legitimate commerce, however, that we can hope to diminish, if not put an end to slavery.

Without minimising the importance of treaty stipulations, we should, nevertheless, place in the strongest light the testimony, that every missionary and traveller has given, that legitimate commerce is the arm to fight with in the struggle with slavery in Africa. The memorial to Lord Granville of the Anti-Slavery Society places this before us in the clearest language.

April 12th.

My Lords,

"The Committee of the British and Foreign Anti-Slavery Society have read, with deep interest, the draft of a treaty with Portugal, for the future regulation and delimitation of her possessions, and of her claims in South-western Africa. While the committee feel grateful to Her Majesty's Government for the careful provisions, they have made in the treaty for the suppression of the slave trade, they nevertheless hold strong

objections to its ratification, on the following grounds:—
1. That the extensive regions already claimed to be occupied by Portugal, have for ages been devoted to the prosecution of the slave trade, both on the part of her own subjects and of Arab marauders. 2. That such subjects of Portugal, as exist in these countries, have been largely supplied by the expatriation of convicts from the mother-country, conducing greatly to the elements of crime and disorder. 3. That long experience has shown, that any control over these regions on the part of the Portuguese Home Government, is of the feeblest character, in consequence of which, the slave trade provisions of this treaty must necessarily, to a large extent, prove ineffective. 4. That in confirmation of these allegations, the committee are able to show, on unquestionable evidence, that at this time the slave trade is, to a considerable amount, being carried on by the Portuguese from their settlements of Loanda to the islands of St. Momé and Principe, and even to the Cape de Verds. Under such conditions, the committee would look with great apprehension on the acknowledgment of any claims on the part of Portugal to any territories which have heretofore been disallowed by Great Britain. Specially would they do so in respect of any claim by Portugal of a jurisdiction over any part of the River Congo. In view of the ineffective and corrupt character of the administration of Portugal in her African territories, the committee are compelled to regard such an occupation as obstructive to any real suppression of the slave trade, and subversive of any hope of its being now supplanted in those regions of Africa by a larger extension of legitimate commerce and of Christian civilisation.

"On behalf of the Anti-Slavery Committee.

"We are, with much respect,

"ARTHUR PEASE (President).

"EDMUND STURGE (Chairman).

"JOSEPH ALLEN (Treasurer).

"CHARLES H. ALLEN (Secretary)."

PART VII.

In conclusion, we are told that one object of the treaty is "To promote the development of commerce and civilisation." With reference to this expression, which is used in the treaty, Mr. Jacob Bright wrote in the *Daily News* of April 18, "The world is familiar with the hollowness and insincerity of diplomatic utterances, but it would be difficult to find a stronger case of insincerity than in the document from which I quote. The Portuguese are to develop commerce and civilisation on the Congo!"

"The general objects which Her Majesty's Government aimed at in the negotiations," to use Lord Granville's words in his letter of March 21, "have been, they believe, fully attained by the present treaty." These objects, after the recognition of Portuguese sovereignty, are stated in his letter to be "to obtain guarantees for the proper treatment of British trade, and for the complete equality, in all matters, of Her Majesty's subjects with those of Portugal, as well as for the treatment of the most favoured nation," the final object being, "to secure that transit through the territory occupied by Portugal should be free as regards all practicable routes."

The questions of sovereignty, and of practicable routes have been already considered.

As regards "proper treatment" of British trade, how is this brought about by obtaining complete equality with the subjects of Portugal? The Portuguese complain of the effect of the duties imposed on trade in the Portuguese African possessions. The trade of the Congo district is, at present, free for all. From a state of freedom from duties to the condition of things under the treaty, is not a "bargain" (whatever Mr. Johnston may have said) to satisfy this country, and is not (in the opinion of the Chambers of Commerce) "proper treatment" of British trade.

At the present moment, we are striving to obtain more favourable terms, where prohibitive tariffs now exist. The Congo district is absolutely free. Does Portugal throw open to us its African ports? This is what Lancashire desires; but such a boon is not to be obtained under the proposed treaty. If anything, even in a small degree, can force down prohibitive duties, and other imposts in the Portuguese African possessions, it is to be effected by maintaining the commercial freedom of the Congo district.

After teaching our methods of manufacture, inculcating free-trade doctrines, and opening our markets, we know it is the consumer that reaps the benefit. The consumer in Africa, however, is not to share this blessing. The introduction of British goods to another country, and that a free country being in question, why is not the most vigorous effort made to continue, wherever it exists, freedom from import duties? There is a prospect, through agencies at present at work, of an extension of the trade that now exists in the Congo district. Shall we deliberately throw away this opening?

The opinion of our mercantile and manufacturing centres has been given. The decision of the Liverpool Chamber of Commerce is adverse to the treaty. The Manchester Chamber of Commerce replied to Lord Granville's letter of March 21st, that "it saw no ground for modifying the views it has so often and so earnestly expressed." The Chambers of Commerce of Manchester, of Birmingham, of Glasgow, of Sheffield, and of Swansea, have all passed resolutions in disapprobation of the treaty, and have petitioned Parliament that it may not be ratified. The Council of the London Chamber of Commerce has recently discussed the Congo treaty and "condemned it as detrimental to British trade."

It is not the Secretary of State, still less the Under Secretary for Foreign Affairs, or the permanent officials, that can be held responsible. It may be said, perhaps, that the negotiations should have been broken off, after the debate last year when Mr. Jacob Bright, Mr. Whitley, Mr. Bourke, Mr. W. E.

Forster, and Sir S. Northcote spoke in opposition to the proposed treaty. But was it not then too late? Could the Government, by its own action, do anything to revoke the important decision on the question of sovereignty which was communicated to Portugal at the earliest stage of the negotiations? Lord Granville informs M. D'Antas on the 15th of December, 1882, that "Her Majesty's Government have given their most careful consideration" to Sen. Serpa's despatch, and that they "would be prepared to enter upon the negotiations of a convention," the first basis of which, as appears in the next line of the despatch, is "that Great Britain should recognise the sovereignty of Portugal."

This despatch is more than the act of the Secretary of State. It is the authoritative expression of the decision, the will, the policy of the Government.

A desire to settle amicably questions and differences that arise between two Powers deserves, and will always win the support and sympathy of the country. Can we, however, say that under all the circumstances of the Congo question, forgetting all the past, we can hand over this free territory to the rule of Portugal?

The treaty has been concluded. The 15th article requires that it shall be ratified, and that the ratifications shall be exchanged at London as soon as possible. The session of the Portuguese Parliament has closed; and it is not likely that there will be any haste in asking for the ratification of the treaty.

The usual course is for treaties to be presented to Parliament after ratification, and it is well for the country that on the present occasion this course has not been followed.

Whenever the treaty, or the further correspondence is discussed in Parliament, the Government will have to explain and defend its policy; and the representatives of the nation will be expected to guard the country's honour, to watch over its commercial interests, and to secure for British trade expansion and development.

NOTES.

NOTE 1.

The necessity for extending our commercial relations and finding new markets for our manufactured goods becomes more and more apparent. That the state of the cotton trade is far from satisfactory may be proved by a reference to the *Economist* for May 10th :—" Speaking generally the cotton trade cannot be said to be one whit better than it was at the close of the year, when the employers were constrained to enforce the reduction of wages. The report of the *British Trade Journal* for April is, that: "Slowly, but surely, the truth is becoming known respecting the cotton trade. The manufacturers have curtailed production, by stopping a portion of the machinery, and have reduced the wages, but neither course has brought relief."

It is satisfactory to see that the Board of Trade Returns for April, 1884, show that the export from Great Britain of articles of cotton manufacture to West Africa is increasing.

Quantities.		*Values.*	
Four months ended April 30th.		Four months ended April 30th.	
West Coast of Africa (British).			
Piece goods, in yards.		West Coast of Africa (British).	
1883.	1884.	1883.	1884.
13,963,200	17,633,400	£170,914	£205,643
West Coast of Africa (Foreign).			
Piece goods, in yards.		West Coast of Africa (Foreign).	
1883.	1884.	1883.	1884.
16,268,900	20,026,000	£218,897	£262,832

NOTE 2.

Lord Granville, in his speech on the Congo Treaty in the House of Lords on May 9th, 1884, said : " It is all very well for individuals to say that we are attacking freedom of trade." The complaint, however, that is made is that as Great Britain is a free trade country, every effort should be made to retain the right, now possessed in the Congo territory, of free admission for British goods.

NOTE 3.

The motives that led former Governments to resist the claims of Portugal are alluded to by Lord Granville in his speech on May 9th. He is reported to have said that the motive of the different Secretaries of State was "exclusively the fear of the Portuguese encouraging, and of our not being able to deal with, the slave trade." In addition to the passages already cited from the correspondence, it may be mentioned that Lord Clarendon, in his despatch to Mr. Howard of May 26th, 1856, says: "I have to instruct you to point out to the Government of His Most Faithful Majesty the embarrassments in which they will be involved by any attempt to interfere with the rights which British subjects have for a long series of years enjoyed of carrying on *a free commercial intercourse* with the natives of the district to the north of Angola."

NOTE 4.

Lord Granville states, in his despatch of March 15th, 1883, that "the claims of Portugal are not established." In his speech on May 9th, 1884, however, he says, "The Portuguese have claimed this particular territory for nearly 400 years, and there is no reason why their claim should not be perfectly good.'' The extent to which the Portuguese claims may be carried can be inferred from a pamphlet (referred to by Lord Granville in his despatch of March 15th, 1883) by the Secretary of the Lisbon Geographical Society, from the English edition of which the following passage is taken: "The Portuguese spread themselves rapidly into the interior of Equatorial Africa, which they pierced and explored in many directions. Merely to continue this brief indication of our discoveries to the south of the Equator, would be equivalent to writing the history of our vast and ancient dominions on the great black Continent." In a letter from "A Portuguese" in the *Morning Post* of May 6th, a map of Africa of the year 1570 is referred to, "in which," the writer says, "is manifest the great extent of the dominion of Portugal in that part of the world, and also the original Portuguese names of the lakes, for which new names have been invented by English explorers." The fame of the Portuguese discoverers of a former day will endure. Imperishable, also, will be the honoured names of the African travellers of the last thirty years, to whom (if we may apply the words of Mr. Keith Johnston in the Preface to Stanford's 'Africa') is due "the rolling back of the clouds of obscurity which until a few years ago hid from view all but the coast line " of Africa.

TREATY WITH PORTUGAL.

Her Majesty the Queen of the United Kingdom of Great Britain and Ireland, Empress of India, &c., &c., &c., and His Most Faithful Majesty the King of Portugal and the Algarves, &c., &c., &c., being animated with the desire to draw closer the ties of friendship which unite the two nations; to put an end to all difficulties relative to the rights of sovereignty over the districts at the mouth of the Congo on the West Coast of Africa, situated between 8° and 5° 12' of south latitude; to provide for the complete extinction of the Slave Trade; and to promote the development of commerce and civilization in the African Continent; have resolved to conclude a Treaty for this purpose, and have named as their Plenipotentiaries, that is to say :

Her Majesty the Queen of the United Kingdom of Great Britain and Ireland, Empress of India, the Right Honourable Granville George, Earl Granville, Lord Leveson, a Peer of the United Kingdom, Knight of the Most Noble Order of the Garter, a Member of Her Majesty's Privy Council, Lord Warden of the Cinque Ports, and Constable of Dover Castle, Chancellor of the University of London, Her Majesty's Principal Secretary of State for Foreign Affairs, &c., &c.;

And His Most Faithful Majesty the King of Portugal and the Algarves, Senhor Miguel Martins d'Antas, a Member of His Majesty's Council, Peer of the Realm, Honorary Minister and Secretary of State, Commander of the Ancient, Most Noble, and Illustrious Order of St. James, for the reward of scientific, literary, and artistic merit, Grand Cross of the Royal Order of Charles the Third of Spain, of Leopold of Belgium, Envoy Extraordinary and Minister Plenipotentiary of His Most Faithful Majesty at the Court of Her Britannic Majesty, &c., &c.;

Who, after having communicated to each other their respective full powers, found in good and due form, have agreed upon the following Articles:

ARTICLE I.

Subject to the conditions of the present Treaty, Her Britannic Majesty agrees to recognise the sovereignty of His Most Faithful Majesty the King of Portugal and the Algarves over that part of the West Coast of Africa situated between 8° and 5° 12' of south latitude; and inland as far as follows :—

On the River Congo the limit shall be Nokki.

On the coast situated between 8° and 5° 12' of south latitude the inland eastern frontier shall coincide with the boundaries of the present possessions of the coast and riparian tribes. This frontier shall be defined, and the definition shall be communicated with the least possible delay by His Most Faithful Majesty to Her Britannic Majesty.

The definition, when approved by the High Contracting Parties, shall be recorded in a Protocol to be annexed to the present Treaty.

ARTICLE II.

The territory specified in Article I. shall be open to all nations, and foreigners of all nationalities whatever, conforming themselves to the laws of the country, shall enjoy within the said territory the same benefits, advantages, and treatment, in every respect, as the subjects of Portugal.

They shall have full liberty to enter, travel, or reside, with their families, in any part of the said territory.

They shall be permitted to establish factories or trading stations; to possess, purchase, rent, or lease land, houses, manufactories, warehouses, shops, and premises, and all other kinds of property.

They shall be allowed to carry on their commerce by wholesale or retail, either in person or by any agents whom they may think fit to employ, and in accordance with the existing local usages and customs of trade.

ARTICLE III.

The High Contracting Parties recognise the entire freedom in respect to commerce and navigation of the Rivers Congo and Zambesi and their affluents for the subjects and flags of all Nations.

The claims of Portugal on the Shire shall not extend beyond the confluence of the River Ruo with that river.

ARTICLE IV.

The trade and navigation of all rivers and waterways within the territory specified in Article I., and along the sea-coast thereof, shall be open to the flags of all nations, and shall not be subject to any monopoly, exclusive concession, or other impediment, nor to any customs duties, tolls, charges, fees, fines, or other imposts whatever not expressly provided for in the present Treaty, or hereafter agreed upon by the High Contracting Parties.

A Mixed Commission, composed of Delegates of Great Britain and Portugal, shall be appointed to draw up Regulations for the navigation, police, and supervision of the Congo and other waterways within the territory specified in Article I., and to watch over their execution.

The Regulations may impose such tolls as may be sufficient to defray the cost of works necessary to facilitate trade and navigation and the expenses of the Commission.

The Commission shall come to an arrangement with the Portuguese authorities for the erection and maintenance of lighthouses, beacons, and marks to denote channels.

ARTICLE V.

No transit or other duties, direct or indirect, of whatever denomination, shall be levied on goods in transit by water through the territory specified in Article I. This freedom from duties shall apply to goods transhipped in course of transit, or landed in bond for further conveyance by water. The transhipment or landing in bond of such goods will be effected under the supervision of the Portuguese authorities, in order to prevent any fraud, and the expenses of such supervision will be chargeable to the traders or their agents. The scale of such charges will be fixed by the Mixed Commission. No such duties shall be levied on goods in transit by land through that territory, which shall have been legally imported and which shall have paid the duties imposed by the Tariff approved by the present Treaty.

ARTICLE VI.

All roads in the territory specified in Article I. now open, or which may hereafter be opened, shall be kept free and open to all travellers and caravans, and for the passage of goods.

ARTICLE VII.

Complete protection shall be afforded to missionaries or other ministers of religion of any Christian denomination, of whatever nation or country, in the exercise of their vocation, within the territory specified in Article I.

They shall not be hindered or molested in their endeavours to teach the doctrines of Christianity to all persons willing and desirous to be taught; nor shall any natives who may embrace any form of Christian faith be on that account, or on account of the teaching or exercise thereof, molested or troubled in any manner whatsoever.

It is further agreed that the local authorities shall set apart a piece of land within a convenient distance of each of the principal towns, to be used as a burial-ground for persons of whatever religious denomination.

All forms of religious worship and religious ordinances shall be tolerated, and no hindrance whatever shall be offered thereto by the Portuguese authorities.

Missionaries of religion, whether natives or foreigners, and religious bodies, shall have a perfect right to erect churches, chapels, schools, and other buildings, which shall be protected by the Portuguese authorities.

All religious establishments, of whatever denomination, shall be on a footing of perfect equality as regards taxation and local charges.

ARTICLE VIII.

Her Britannic Majesty engages to communicate to His Most Faithful Majesty immediately after the ratification of the present Treaty, all Treaties or Engagements subsisting between Great Britain and native Chiefs in the territory specified in Article I.

His Most Faithful Majesty engages to communicate to Her Britannic Majesty all Treaties or Engagements subsisting between Portugal and native Chiefs in the said territory.

His Most Faithful Majesty engages to respect and confirm all the rights of the native Chiefs and of the inhabitants of the said territory under any of the Treaties and Engagements above mentioned, so far as is compatible with the sovereignty of Portugal; and undertakes to protect and maintain the said Chiefs and inhabitants in the free possession and enjoyment of the lands and other property now held by them, and not to allow them to suffer on account of anything which has happened in the past.

ARTICLE IX.

The Customs Tariff in the territory specified in Article I. shall not, for the term of ten years from the date of the exchange of the ratifications of the present Treaty, exceed that which was adopted in the Province of Mozambique in the year 1877. At the end of that term the Tariff may be revised, with the consent of the two High Contracting Parties; but no alteration shall be made therein pending such revision.

Provided always that, in the territory specified in Article I. of the present Treaty, British ships shall not at any time hereafter be liable to the payment of any higher or other duties and charges, or be subject to any other restrictions, than are there payable or imposed on Portuguese ships; and goods, whether the property of British subjects, or imported in British vessels, or of British origin or manufacture, shall not at any time hereafter be subject to any differential treatment whatsoever, but shall be on the same footing in every respect as goods the property of Portuguese subjects, or imported in Portuguese vessels, or the produce or manufacture of Portugal.

Such equality of treatment shall apply to British vessels and goods, from whatever port or place arriving, and whatever may be their place of destination.

In all the African possessions of Portugal the present Customs Tariff shall not be raised for the term of ten years from the date of the exchange of the ratifications of the present Treaty.

No bill of health or other quarantine formality shall be required in any Portuguese port from British ships bound direct for British ports.

ARTICLE X.

His Most Faithful Majesty guarantees to British subjects and their commerce in all the African possessions of Portugal, in addition to any rights which they may already possess in the Portuguese Colonies, the treatment of the most favoured third nation:—

1. As regards residence, whether temporary or permanent; the exercise of

any calling or profession; the payment of taxes or other imposts; and the enjoyment of all legal rights and privileges, including the acquiring, holding, and power of disposing of property.

2. As regards commerce; in respect of import and export duties and all other charges on or in respect of goods of whatever description, and whatever may be their place of origin or manufacture, and whether intended for consumption, warehousing, or re-exportation. Also with respect to the transit of goods, prohibition of importation, exportation, or transit; samples, Customs formalities, and all other matters connected with commerce and trade.

3. As regards navigation; in respect of vessels, whether steam or sailing, from whatever place arriving, and whatever may be the place of origin or destination of their cargoes. Also, in respect of all charges or dues on or in respect of the said vessels and cargoes, and all formalities and regulations relative to them.

4. Any favour, privilege, or immunity in regard to subjects, commerce, or navigation, as well as any reduction of Customs duties or other charges on or in respect of goods or vessels which may hereafter be conceded by Portugal to any third Power, shall be extended immediately and unconditionally to Great Britain.

5. British Consular officers, as regards appointment, residence, functions, and privileges, shall be placed on the footing of the most favoured nation.

ARTICLE XI.

Every assistance shall be given by the local authorities in all the African possessions of Portugal to vessels wrecked on the coasts or in the rivers, or forced into the ports or the entrance of rivers by stress of weather.

Such vessels and their cargoes shall be exempt from all Customs duties, charges, fees, fines, and other imposts whatever, except as regards any goods landed therefrom for purposes of sale or barter.

Information of such wrecks shall be given, without delay, to the nearest British Consular officer, who shall be authorised to interpose for the protection of the ship, its merchandise, and effects.

ARTICLE XII.

The Portuguese legislation for the complete extinction of slavery and the Treaties for the suppression of the Slave Trade shall, from the date of the exchange of the ratifications of the present Treaty, be effectively applied to the territory specified in Article I.

The High Contracting Parties bind themselves to use all possible means for the purpose of finally extinguishing slavery and the Slave Trade on the eastern and western coasts of Africa.

His Most Faithful Majesty agrees to grant, from the date of the ratification of the present Treaty, permission to Her Britannic Majesty's ships employed in suppressing the Slave Trade to enter the bays, ports, creeks, rivers, and other places in the eastern African Colonies or possessions of Portugal where no Portuguese authorities shall be established, and to prevent the Slave Trade from being carried on in such places. British vessels employed in this service shall exercise all the powers conferred on Her Majesty's vessels by the Slave Trade Treaty between Great Britain and Portugal of the 3rd July, 1842.

Similar powers shall be given, if required, for similar purposes to Portuguese vessels in Her Britannic Majesty's South African dominions.

Whenever the Commander of a cruizer of one of the High Contracting Parties shall have occasion to act under the provisions of this Article in the territorial waters of the other High Contracting Party, such Commander shall, whenever practicable, having regard to the circumstances of the case, invite a naval or other officer of the other High Contracting Party to accompany the expedition, in order to represent the national flag in such territorial waters.

The provisions of this Article shall come into force immediately on the exchange of the ratifications of the present Treaty, except as regards any provision which may be found to require legislative sanction in either country, and as regards such provision, it shall come into force from the date when such legislative sanction shall have been obtained and duly notified by the High Contracting Party requiring the same to the other High Contracting Party.

ARTICLE XIII.

The provisions of the present Treaty, affecting the territory specified in Article I., shall be fully applied to all territories adjoining the same in Africa that may hereafter be brought under the sovereignty of His Most Faithful Majesty the King of Portugal and the Algarves.

ARTICLE XIV.

His Most Faithful Majesty the King of Portugal and the Algarves engages for himself, his heirs and successors, that if at any time it shall be the intention of Portugal to withdraw from the fort of St. John the Baptist of Ajudá, on the coast of Mina, due notification of such intention shall be given to Great Britain, to whom the cession of the fort, and of all rights appertaining to its possession, shall be offered; and no arrangement shall be made for the cession of the fort to any other Power without the previous consent of Great Britain.

This engagement shall apply in all its terms to the abandonment or cession by Portugal of any rights which may be claimed by her between 5° east and 5° west longitude on the same coast.

ARTICLE XV.

The present Treaty shall be ratified, and the ratifications shall be exchanged at London as soon as possible.

In witness whereof the respective Plenipotentiaries have signed the present Treaty, and have affixed thereto the seals of their arms.

Done in duplicate at London the twenty-sixth day of February, in the year of our Lord one thousand eight hundred and eighty-four.

(Signed)   GRANVILLE,

MIGUEL MARTINS D'ANTAS.

PRINTED BY EDWARD STANFORD, 55, CHARING CROSS, LONDON, S.W